# Diplomacy
## Makes a Difference

UNITED NATIONS ⚛ NATIONS UNIES

Elizabeth Anderson Lopez

## Consultants

**Crystal Hahm**
*Tustin Unified School District*

**Bijan Kazerooni, M.A.**
*Chapman University*

## Publishing Credits

Rachelle Cracchiolo, M.S.Ed., *Publisher*
Conni Medina, M.A.Ed., *Managing Editor*
Emily R. Smith, M.A.Ed., *Series Developer*
June Kikuchi, *Content Director*
Susan Daddis, M.A.Ed., *Editor*
Courtney Roberson, *Senior Graphic Designer*

**Image Credits:** p.8 Fiji's Department of Information/Xinhua/
Alamy Live News; p.9 Win McNamee/Getty Images; p.12
(insert) NASA; p.15 White House Photo/Alamy; p.18 Mark
J Sullivan/Pacific Press/LightRocket via Getty Images; p.19
Agung Samosir/Pacific Press/LightRocket via Getty Images;
p.20 Ronald Reagan Presidential Library, National Archives
and Records; p.21 Drew Angerer/Getty Images; p.24 Mark
Reinstein/Alamy; p.25, 32 U.S. National Archives; all other
images from iStock and/or Shutterstock.

### Library of Congress Cataloging-in-Publication Data

Names: Lopez, Elizabeth Anderson, author.
Title: Diplomacy makes a difference / Elizabeth Anderson Lopez.
Description: Huntington Beach, CA : Teacher Created Materials, [2018] |
    Includes index. | Audience: K to Grade 3.
Identifiers: LCCN 2017053279 (print) | LCCN 2018006115 (ebook) | ISBN
    9781425825607 | ISBN 9781425825188 (pbk.)
Subjects: LCSH: Diplomacy--Juvenile literature. | International
    relations--Juvenile literature.
Classification: LCC JZ1305 (ebook) | LCC JZ1305 .L66 2018 (print) | DDC
    327.2--dc23
LC record available at https://lccn.loc.gov/2017053279

### Teacher Created Materials

5301 Oceanus Drive
Huntington Beach, CA 92649-1030
www.tcmpub.com

**ISBN 978-1-4258-2518-8**

© 2018 Teacher Created Materials, Inc.

# Table of Contents

# How the World Works Together

The world is a big place. There are a lot of countries. In fact, there are almost two hundred countries. Many of them have their own languages, **cultures**, foods, clothing, and more. How do they work together?

It takes a lot of work. It involves **diplomacy**. It requires rules. Some rules are written to keep people safe. Other rules make sure everyone is treated fairly. There are many groups that have rules for countries to follow.

# Leaders and Laws

Each country has a leader. It is a big job. Leaders work hard. Good leaders have things in common. They are honest and fair. They make choices that are hard. They help make laws.

In many countries, people choose their leaders. They do this by voting. Leaders do not always have the same title. In the United States, the leader is called the president. In England, the leader is called the prime minister.

## Diplomats at Work

Diplomats are men and women who represent their countries. Some diplomats work in **embassies**. They meet with leaders and diplomats from other countries. They work to solve problems. These include things such as **trade**, safety, and keeping peace.

This is the embassy of Canada in Washington, DC.

## Passing Laws

Countries have rules. These rules are called *laws*. They tell people how to be good **citizens**. Laws tell us what is legal and not legal. People who are caught breaking a law might get in trouble. They may have to face **consequences**.

These leaders work to pass laws.

In the United States, Congress makes and passes laws. There are 535 members of Congress. Groups that make laws come in all sizes. In some countries, fewer than 20 people make the laws.

The U.S. Congress meets to hear a speech.

## Breaking Laws

Sadly, people break laws. Most countries have ways to deal with this. Many use courts with a judge or **jury**. These people listen and decide if a person is guilty of a crime. A judge or a jury also decides how to punish people.

A judge listens to people in court.

People who are found guilty of crimes are not given the same punishments. That is because not all crimes are the same. A person might get a ticket for speeding. But if someone steals a car, he or she might get sent to jail.

A police officer pulls a driver over for speeding.

# Crimes Between Countries

What if a citizen of one country breaks a law in a different country? How does that work? It can be hard to figure out. The most important thing is for the countries to work together.

## Who Owns Outer Space?

Each country has its own borders. But who owns planets? Can a country say Jupiter belongs to it? In 1967, world leaders said no. They worked together to make this decision. They also agreed that more than one country can explore space.

**International Space Station**

CAPE VERDE

THE GA

GUINE

VENEZUELA

GUYANA

COLOMBIA

SURINAME

French Guiana (FRANCE)

ECUADOR

PERU

BRAZIL

BOLIVIA

PARAGUAY

Laws may not be the same in different countries. The leaders and courts may need to get involved. They need to figure out the right thing to do to be fair. They may need to **compromise**.

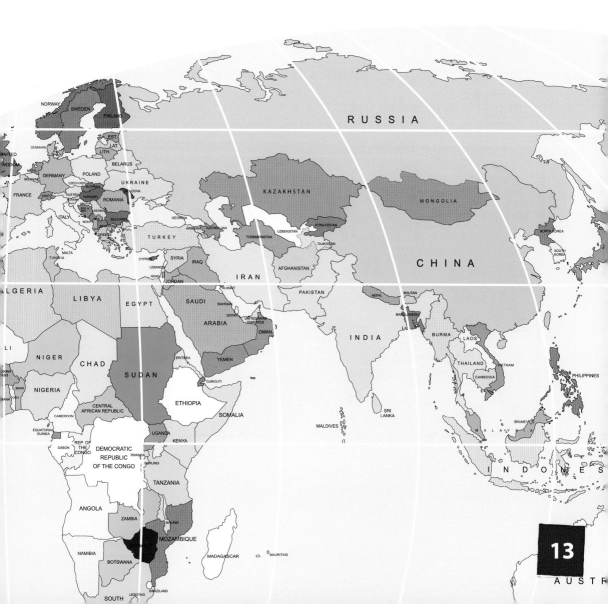

# How Nations Solve Problems

What happens when there are problems between students at school? For example, if a friend is bullied, you want to help. But you don't know what to do. You might bring up the problem during a class meeting. Other students might give good ideas to stop the bullying.

Just like students, countries sometimes have problems. When countries have **issues**, their leaders may need to help solve them.

Students hold a class meeting to help fix problems.

There are global groups that can help. They listen to all sides. They try to be fair. These **global** groups also work to make sure that people have clean water, food, and good health care. They help keep peace and protect people around the world.

United Nations building

## Role of the United Nations

The United Nations (UN) is a group of countries that help keep peace in the world. There are close to two hundred member countries. The UN does not pass laws. It votes on rules. These rules support peace among countries.

United Nations meeting

## A Special Flag

The U.N. flag shows two things. One is a circular world map as seen from the North Pole. It also has a wreath of olive branches. They are a symbol of peace.

The UN also works to help solve other problems around the world. For example, it helps countries that do not have water that is safe to drink.

## More Groups Around the Globe

There are many groups that help the whole world. Some of them are part of the UN.

One of those groups helps children. It is called UNICEF. It raises money to help kids learn and stay healthy. It has helped many children around the world.

A diplomat from Kenya works to help children.

The World Health Organization (WHO) is also part of the UN. It is a group that works on health issues all over the world. Some countries do not have medicine. The WHO makes sure they get what they need to help their citizens.

The WHO gives children medicine to keep them healthy.

Ronald Reagan meets with the
leader of the Soviet Union.

## Meeting One on One

Leaders also meet face-to-face. This is to help their countrie
work together to solve problems. Many U.S. presidents have
done this. Ronald Reagan met with the head of the Soviet Union
They worked together. They helped build peace.

Barack Obama works with the leader of Colombia.

Barack Obama went to many countries. He met with many of their leaders. These leaders worked with him to try and solve world issues.

# Global Issues

Countries work with one another to solve issues. One of these issues includes free trade. That means countries can trade items with other countries.

## Fair Trade

Fair trade is practiced around the world. It makes sure that people get paid a fair amount for their goods. With fair trade, less-wealthy countries can help themselves.

This ship carries goods that are traded between countries.

# Free Trade

Sometimes, one country has an item another country wants. For example, what if a country does not grow fruit. What does it do? It can buy fruit from other countries. Free trade can make that happen.

Besides food, many other things are traded. Oil, steel, and coal are traded. The World Trade Organization (WTO) makes sure trades are fair. It protects small countries from being bullied by big ones.

# Treaties

When countries make agreements, they write them down. These agreements are often called **treaties**. They can cover many things.

Two or more countries can be part of a treaty. Countries might sign a treaty after they fight. It says that the war is over. Countries also sign treaties about human rights.

The leaders of Israel and Palestine shake hands after signing a treaty.

Treaties are special. They are often signed in front of a crowd. They are sent to the UN. This makes them official. More than 560 treaties have been filed!

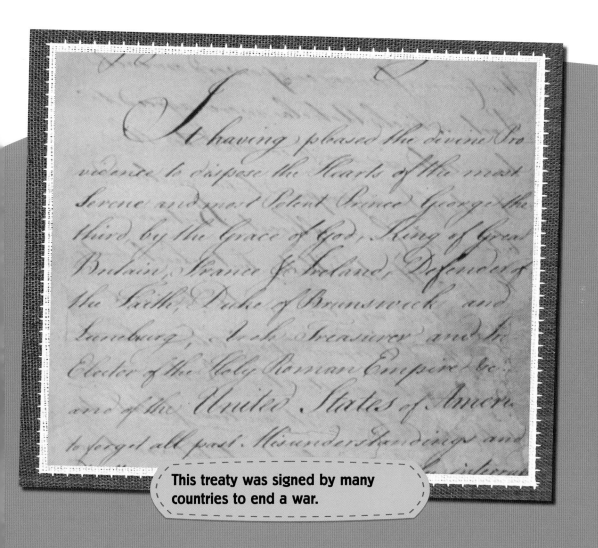

This treaty was signed by many countries to end a war.

# Diplomacy at Work

It is important for countries to solve problems. That keeps their citizens safe. World leaders and diplomats must work to make sure this happens. The UN should step in when needed, too. The UN helps keep peace around the world. It also protects people in times of war or disasters.

The UN helps people around the world.

Free trade and treaties form good relationships between countries. There are fewer problems about what is fair.

All people play a role in keeping peace throughout the world. You can start small. Take part in class meetings. Help a friend solve a problem. These little steps will add up to something bigger!

## Mind Your Manners!

Visitors have to be sensitive to other countries' customs. They may not be what they are used to. In the United States, people greet each other with firm handshakes. Some people in other countries think firm handshakes are rude. They like a loose grip. In some countries, people do not shake hands. They bow to each other instead.

# Journal It!

Imagine you are going to a new country for the first time. What would you want the local people to know about your country? What items would you bring to best represent your country? Find or draw pictures of things that represent your country. Put them in a journal that you can show to the people you meet.

Save some blank pages at the end. Write three questions you would like to ask the people you meet about their country.

# Glossary

**citizens**—people who live in a city, state, or country

**compromise**—to give something up that you want in order to reach an agreement

**consequences**—the results of someone's actions

**cultures**—the beliefs and ways of groups of people

**diplomacy**—the work that helps countries keep or build good relationships

**embassies**—buildings where leaders work in countries that are not their own

**global**—involving the whole world

**issues**—important topics or problems

**jury**—a group of people chosen to make decisions in court

**trade**—the buying and selling of goods between people or countries

**treaties**—agreements made between two or more countries

# Index

# Your Turn!

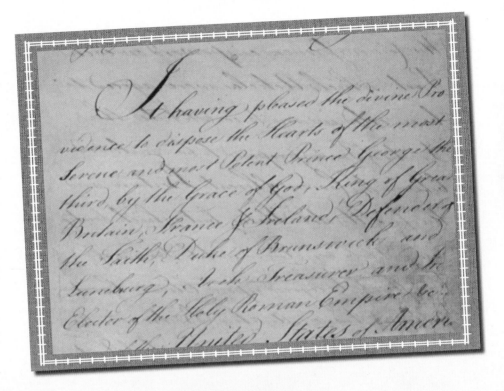

## Making Peace

The treaty above helped the United States gain its independence from England. Think of a problem you have with a friend. Write a treaty to solve the problem. Meet with your friend to talk about the treaty. Sign it if you both agree on how to solve your problem.